*To the Rincon and Village Meadows Church families
for giving me the grace to be their Pastor*

THE JOURNAL I NEVER KEPT – WHAT IF…?

ISBN: 9798711103219

Cover Photo: Lightning over Village Meadows Baptist Church, Sierra Vista, AZ

Acknowledgements

It should go without saying that Jesus Christ is the reason for anyone to write a journal about the ebb and flow of ministry. After all, he is the One who is faithful and true. It is he who equips and empowers us for ministry. But of course, the Lord uses people through whom much of his work in our lives is accomplished. No one has had more of an influence on my ministry than my wife Nancy. Without question she has been God's primary source of refinement in my otherwise naïve view of life and ministry.

I also hold a debt of gratitude to Gale Trow, who has been a partner in ministry with me for nearly two decades. His willingness to be a listening ear and voice of reason has been an invaluable contribution to my longevity at Village Meadows Baptist Church, Sierra Vista, Arizona.

Of course, I could go on naming a host of names recalling those God has used to bless, encourage, strengthen and motivate me but to name a few would leave a host of others not mentioned. I will have to rely on the fact that God knows their names and will reward them accordingly.

I also want to thank God for the members of Rincon Baptist Church in Tucson, Arizona, who took a chance on me in early 1990 and gave me the much needed grace every new pastor needs to survive those critical first years as a lead pastor. I had a remarkable six and a half years there. And then God opened the door for me to return to where it all pretty much began for me in vocational ministry—Sierra Vista. When I married my bride in 1984 I told her that my wish would be to someday retire in Sierra Vista. It was there I began my full-time ministry as the youth pastor at First Baptist Church in early 1978 and I was very blessed to serve in that church for nearly three years.

It would be the end of 1996, a mere sixteen years after I left Sierra Vista, when God would bless me and my family with the opportunity to minister in that town again. This time it would be through the Village Meadows Baptist Church. An incredible congregation that have, much like Rincon, allowed me to grow and lead as their pastor.

It is from these many saints that God has taught me much about what it takes to shepherd God's people for His glory. I thank God in every remembrance of them. I certainly have not deserved their grace and following of my leadership. Thank you Jesus!

Mark Pitts

February 2021

I would like to add a note of appreciation to Sharon Burks, Gale Trow, Keith Henry, David Johnson,

and Fred and Judy Girth for their invaluable feedback on
the early drafts of this book.

TABLE OF CONTENTS

What if…

My intention for putting together this compilation of "what ifs" is that those pastors and church leaders who read this will be encouraged and hopefully garner some helpful insights. At the very least gain some new perspective on old paradigms. Ultimately this brief trip through many of my pastoral experiences will hopefully stimulate one's thinking rather than be merely informational or even entertaining. I am not looking for a consensus and neither am I trying to tell the reader where he or she may be erring. I do not expect you to agree with all my conclusions whether philosophical or theological. That is, and has always been, for you to discern in your own walk with Christ and study of Scripture.

The title, *The Journal I Never Kept*, is more of a confession and not a recommendation. I wish that I had developed the habit of journaling early in my pastorate as that would have given me vastly more information from which to draw from instead of my diminishing memory. None-the-less, this is an effort at recalling the most memorable and pivotal events in my vocational ministry.

My intention for those lay persons who read this is to see a little of what goes on in your pastor's heart. To hopefully recognize the process of decision making along with the mistakes that come from being human as well as the grace that comes from relying on God.

Finally, my intention for everyone who reads this is that you will be blessed with a desire to let all that you do be to the glory of God and the advancement of the Gospel of Jesus Christ.

As you can see, the title of this little chapter is tongue and cheek. What else are we called to shepherd except other humans? My point is simply this—in the day to day challenges of vocational ministry it is all too easy to get caught up in focusing on a strategy, a plan, or one's agenda and forget with whom we are dealing. When we lose sight of the fact that we are to be leading God's sheep out of harm's way and to green pastures, we will quickly get derailed by the frustration that comes when these sheep act in ways that strangely appear to be human like. You know, when they begin to "challenge" your leadership instead of being in lock-step with your every command.

A common mistake pastors young in the ministry make is to lose sight of the central purpose of their calling, which is to shepherd God's flock. Often the "young in ministry" pastor (not all new pastors are young) will take all that "learnin" gained in Seminary or the latest, greatest book or idea, and attempt to force feed the sheep. Invariably this happens when we focus only on what we deem best for the mission of the church and do not invite input from the members.

The culprit that is often behind this shortsightedness is our own ego and pride in that we do not want to modify or change what we have personally concluded is best for the church. This is often manifested in our defensiveness when members do not buy into what we're claiming to be God's will. When we have taken on this kind of attitude we have set ourselves up for personal disappointment, frustration and even anger at those who do not fall right in line behind us.

From time to time when pastors get together there is a tendency to talk about our "problem" sheep. Never by name, but in understandable terms because of our common experiences. Oh, how I wish that when I started pastoring I knew then what I know now; that most of the time the "problem" member is that way because I have failed to sit down and have a heart to heart conversation with them. So many times resistance to a pastor's leadership is nothing more than the consequences of failing to communicate leading to a misunderstanding. A key to having members embrace your leadership is to lead them to take ownership of what you are asking of them. Good communication is a must for this to happen. If any misunderstanding is not addressed early it tends to deteriorate into both parties digging in their heals leading to an "OK Corral" event.

The apostle Paul touches on this human distinctive of pridefulness when he describes for us in 1st Corinthians chapter one the "type" of people God saves. In essence, Paul tells us in verses 26-31 that God saves the simpleton to preach the Gospel to the self-acclaimed intellectual. When you study that text you find that the key distinction in Paul's observation is faith and humility.

Faith and humility must be the ever present attitude and practice of those who give leadership in the Lord's church. When those become lacking the default is to become prideful and territorial and rely solely on human reason. While we are human and will reason as such, it is critical to note that when separated from a humble submission to the Lordship of Christ, human reasoning will cause one to count themselves as the source of their own truth and authority. And, oh, how defensive we can become when we have arrived at that place of great pride.

The temptation to grab the reins from Jesus and begin to *think of ourselves more highly than we ought* (Romans 12:3) plagues us all. Even the pastor! The truth of the matter is that whenever a pastor begins to think of himself as the king of the hill, he is about to fall off that hill. We are where we are only by the grace of God that sustains us in this service of pastoral ministry. The same could be said for any capacity in which God calls and equips. Humble servant leadership is the critical component of being any kind of leader in the household of faith. Paul makes this impeccably clear in his letter to the Philippians (particularly chapter two).

This chapter on shepherding humans is to point out how we all have a penchant for independence from the shepherd. Even the pastor who is the under-shepherd to Jesus, can suffer from independence from the Shepherd.

Such a reality should keep us sober and less reactive to our members when they do not "fall in line" with our thinking, or even rebel against our leadership. Just as God patiently works with us to get us where He wants us to be and to lead from, so, too, should we be patient with those who are being asked to follow us.

Much, much more could be addressed here, but suffice it to say that communication is the key. To get clarity on what you believe God is telling you there must be exhaustive communication with those whom God has called you to lead. Communicating, in what may seem *ad nauseam*, is the only way you will rightly discern God's leading and simultaneously help those you are leading to understand. This takes time. Often more time than you want to take, and regularly requiring more patience than you want to exert. Regardless, you must prayerfully and deliberately take your time all the while communicating with those whom God has placed in your care. As my late father-in-law used to say, "Do not rush the monkey if you want to see a good show!" So, communicate, communicate, communicate—because you are leading humans and, more importantly, you are human, too.

One final observation is needed here. When there is a resistance to your leadership and you have done your best to communicate with them as well as made sure you are pursuing God's will and not your own, then it is safe to conclude that the push-back is against God and His will for them personally. That can be expected when you work with humans. My point is that we must diligently work at making sure we are pursuing humble servant leadership while trusting God to move in the hearts of His people. And yes, even those who are being difficult. I'll say a little more about this later.

So, what if you're called to pastor humans? What changes in attitude or practice are you willing to make to ensure you keep the precious souls you are leading clearly in view?

What I consider a core value, and at the heart of what it means to be a man of integrity, is that you keep the commitments you make. At times that can be very difficult, especially when everything in you (your humanness) tells you to cut and run; or just quietly leave. I do not know of any pastor who has not been faced with the strong temptation to pack up and call it quits. Another one of those confessions we pastors make to one another is how we craft our letter of resignation practically every Sunday on our drive home. Particularly when we feel we just preached the best sermon of our career and no one commented. It is in those moments I confess to Jesus that it is He I wish to please.

Vocational ministry is hard. For that matter, any kind of ministry can be hard at times. But, the challenge unique to the vocational pastor is that he is specifically called by the Holy Spirit through human mediation to a specific church family or ministry. That calling must be clearly ordained. That is to say, it must be clear to all parties involved that this leading of God is His undeniable will. This is of vital importance because without such holy assurances the temptation to quit at the first sign of difficulty is rather significant.

Within this conversation is the issue of integrity I mentioned before. I have never taken a ministry position, whether support staff or as senior pastor, that I did not believe it was God's will. And because of that my genuine intent was to stay in that ministry position as long as I possibly could, and that I would not consider leaving until it became perfectly clear that God was inviting me to move on. It is because of this commitment that I have been blessed to have served in only a few churches since God called me to vocational ministry in 1973.

I wish I could say that this kind of commitment has minimized the number of times I have been tempted to leave. There have been numerous times over the years that I have wished I was somewhere else or even doing something else. Practically all of these temptations have come on the heels of something harsh being said to me or something done in opposition to me. To a lesser degree they also come when I do not see any real fruit from my efforts. This is why I have confessed a number of times in sermons that I have a grass backyard so I can see some immediate gratification when I mow it!

The first test at what I am talking about naturally came in my first substantial vocational position as a youth pastor. In that circumstance the pastor had become difficult to work with following the relocation of the church. I was single at the time and immature in dealing with criticism. It did not help that I had enjoyed a nearly three year-long fruitful ministry with virtually no conflict. I was not smart enough at the time to seek wise counsel and some intervention. I am convinced I would have enjoyed a few more years there had I not overreacted. But, I "conveniently" heard the Lord telling me to return to my seminary pursuits which enabled me to put the blame on God. However, when it came time for me to arrive at the seminary I could not bring myself to do it and ended up working in the computer industry in Houston, Texas. This would lead to my absence from vocational ministry for nearly four years.

That is enough of the outcome from being impatient. What about the outcome of being patient in the face of conflict. I would learn this valuable lesson in spades while in my first pastorate. I had enjoyed a wonderful following to my leadership for the first three years I was at Rincon Baptist Church. But then it happened. I was met with some push-back. Keep in mind that I am still relatively young to the pastorate and learning some valuable lessons. Especially the need to learn how important it is to communicate regularly and vigorously. Even though the push-back was inconsequential it caused me to consider how much longer God wanted me to stay in at that particular church and ministry.

That incident motivated me to prayerfully seek God's direction. What He instructed me to do was prepare my resume, but to do nothing with it. So I did and prayed; and prayed; and prayed. I was not sure if God wanted me to do something else in ministry, although there were not many options. I had already been a youth pastor, a music pastor, and even a custodian. I had even earned a Master's degree in preparation for becoming an administrator or education guy, but God closed those doors decisively. God was not calling me to any of those pursuits. All He was calling me to do was be faithful where I was and wait on Him. I did and God continued to bless our ministry at Rincon. But there was still this feeling that one day He was going to move us on.

And so God did, three and a half years after I put together my resume. It would be during those years of waiting that God would test my resolve. While there would still be some varied kinds of conflict that would occur, they were all a part of what it means to shepherd a flock, and, yes, work with humans. As you may have already concluded, having someone challenge your decision making and thus question your leadership is just a part of the ministry. While it still stings my pride, it does not cause me to go "chicken little." This is a good thing and it has enabled me to stay where I am for a long tenure.

On that note, much has been written about the advantages of staying the course with a congregation for a reasonable time. Often, something is said about the "honeymoon period" where the church is all giddy over their new pastor, but how short-lived that can be before the first push-back occurs. Ask any married couple how this works. It is the same in ministry. It is much like he forgets to put down the toilet lid. You know what comes next.

Along with the mysterious honeymoon period is what some observers claim is the amount of time it takes for a congregation to actually accept their pastor as trustworthy. That is putting it bluntly. The more tender way of saying it is that the congregation needs for him to prove to them that they can trust him to be there for them. They need to feel confident he will not just earn their trust and win their hearts, then up and leave them at the "altar." Those who write about such things state that it takes at least five years for this kind of bonding and trust to happen. I cannot confirm that from my own experience because I have been blessed to have been accepted and considered trustworthy very early on in my two pastorates. That may have more to do with who was in that position before me. I did not have to walk into a pastorate where there were ruined relationships everywhere by unresolved conflicts with a previous pastor.

I do not believe that I am somebody special or have God's favor over anyone else. Perhaps my fortune in having longevity is due to my determination to walk through the difficulties that come in ministry instead of using them as an excuse to leave. Been there, done that. And maybe my efforts at communicating with my members have helped a little even though I think I still have a lot of improvement to do in that area.

By the way, when God says *wait* He is up to something. Particularly, He is up to teaching you something which is why it is critical you pray hard and seek wise counsel. The truth be known, much of the time a crisis is simply God's teachable moment to grow you some more.

So, what if God tells you He has another assignment, but to wait? Our walk with Christ is always one of faith and the desire to do His will above all else. Do not be afraid to take a relatively small step of faith and then realize all He is wanting from you at that time is that small step.

What if...God tells you to relocate?

For good reason many parishioners view their pastors as self-serving; of being guilty of personal kingdom building. They arrive at this suspicion because too often the pastor is, in fact, guilty of that. Back to that human pride thing. If a man of God is genuinely interested in reaching the lost and making disciples he will naturally seek to build God's kingdom. But sometimes he can get caught up in a wonder-lust to be like that "successful" church down the street or in the next town, etc. It takes some maturing, but eventually a pastor will come to the conclusion that what God wants for the church he leads is not what God has given to that other church. For this reason the wise pastor will organize and lead his congregation to seek God's specific plan for them. Rest assured that at the heart of it will be the reaching of the lost and the discipleship of the saved. How that is to be accomplished is according to God's specific directive.

Soon after I arrived at Village Meadows the first thing I felt we needed to do was to get some clarity as to what God was leading the church to be and become. They were in a relatively new sanctuary and were experiencing good attendance and healthy attitudes. We organized a long-range vision team of 12 members with the previous interim pastor facilitating it. Of course, I was one of the team members. We met frequently over a period of months seeking to discern God's will. We were asking difficult questions that required much prayer and further discussion. Fundamentally, our choices had come down to the question of relocation or having a church planting strategy. The latter would be where we would organize a portion of our congregation to go out and start a new church.

Ultimately, the team elected to propose we relocate in order to grow larger and, thereby, accomplish more in God's Kingdom to include church planting. I can honestly say that I did not influence the vision team's conclusion. I purposefully avoided giving into the idea of a bigger and better campus. For Pete's sake, at the time, we were sitting in the newest and most beautiful sanctuary in the city!

While a vision team made up of well-respected church members can recommend to the congregation they relocate there is no guarantee they will go along with it. The real test for us was when we convened a special called business meeting on the third anniversary of being in the new sanctuary (one they had built themselves with the aid of Baptist Builders). The proverbial fleece would be in their willingness to move away from such a nice facility. Some things are so clearly God at work you do not even need to discuss it. They voted unanimously to relocate. There was actually one individual out of the 100 present who voted against it. He approached me afterwards to tell me why he was against it (I did not know who because we voted by secret ballot). Essentially he had a question that had yet to be answered. When I answered

it, he immediately said, "Well, in that case I am for it."
Once again we cannot underestimate the importance of
good communication.

The significance of what I am pointing out here is
that when God tells you to relocate it must be Him
speaking to the whole and not just the leader dictating
what he believes God is saying. Some of this goes into the
sobering statistic that 80% of the pastors who lead a
church to relocate or go through a building program leave
after the move or build is complete. One of the reasons for
this is that when the pastor has had to "convince" the
church to make the move or do the build it is more his
idea than theirs. Invariably he will end up dragging the
members toward the finish line and in so doing create a
good deal of friction. Friction that causes him to suddenly
hear God's call to move. When it is the whole
congregation making the decision (there is that ownership
thing again) it makes the target on the pastor's back much
smaller.

Right after the church had elected to relocate we
organized a team to search out possible locations for us to
move. I immediately called a pastor friend in Tucson who
had just led his congregation in a relocation of their
campus—their very large campus. They go by the name
Casas. My pastor friend advised me to secure the services
of a master planner and then he added that the average
length of time it takes to relocate is ten years. I did not
want to hear that. Remember what I said earlier about the

necessity of waiting on God and being patient. Do you want to guess how long it took before we were fully moved to our new campus? You got it! Ten years.

Please understand that when God tells you to relocate He is not doing so to make your life miserable or abandon you along the way. Time and time again God has proven Himself faithful to His directive for the Village Meadows family to relocate.

By the way, as of the writing of this chapter, we are under way in the building of the fourth phase of our construction on the now not so new campus.

So, what if God tells you and your church to relocate? First of all make absolutely certain the rest of the congregation is hearing the same thing! With that you can lead them to walk into the challenges that come with such a divine directive. Do not miss the obvious truth that where God directs He equips. That is to say, when God directs you to relocate He knows exactly how He plans to provide the resources for you to do that—principally through the church family.

As remarkable as it may seem it is not a given that a church who studies the Bible will learn biblical stewardship. Statistically, most churches do not understand biblical stewardship. The likelihood of that is due to the lie that has permeated much of the church growth chatter that says the average seeker is turned off by what appears to be the church always asking for money. Granted, there are those few churches that go overboard and make their ministry one of "name it and claim it" or use guilt to coerce people to give.

You may already be aware that the Scriptures have more to say about stewardship than almost every other subject. And while stewardship is only a part of the spectrum of what it means to be a disciple of Jesus Christ it is without a doubt a critical component in what it means to truly surrender to the Lordship of Christ. As such, teaching the congregation a balanced diet of what the Bible says on stewardship is essential. I have to confess that early in my pastorate I had decided no one would have grounds to complain about the church I pastored asking for money "all the time." So, I decided a good once a year stewardship message would do the trick. How naïve.

I mentioned earlier the evidences of God's faithfulness to carry out His directive for us to relocate.

One of these evidences was when I received a phone call from a state convention staff member telling me he had jointly developed a biblical stewardship training manual and wanted to know if I was interested in having him come and share it with our congregation. His name was Bill May and I thank God that I said yes to his offer. Little did I know that the day long Sunday event where Bill shared what the Bible says about stewardship, would be God preparing His people to achieve remarkable things through an understanding of biblical stewardship.

The Sunday Bill taught us was a mere three months after the church voted to relocate. Five months later we launched the first of two stewardship campaigns. God simply prepared us for that. It is important to note that if you want to succeed with fund raising through a stewardship campaign it must be a congregational decision. When the proposal was made for us to enter such a campaign it was much better received because God had faithfully brought us a servant a few months prior to prepare our hearts with the Word of God on stewardship.

If you know anything about stewardship campaigns they involve organizing various teams to carry out different aspects of the campaign. In our case we were blessed to have a campaign director who was a retired pastor and had been leading churches in these kinds of events. It did not hurt that he had been the interim pastor before my arrival. And, yes, the same man who facilitated our long-range vision team. His name was Gene Laird. I repeat, God's faithfulness is apparent all along the journey.

Stewardship campaigns are typically three years in duration with donors giving toward their pledge with the goal of completing it at the end of the campaign. It is from these pledges that decisions are made as to how to proceed. In our case we were simply raising money to buy whatever property God was going to lead us.

A main component of any stewardship campaign is the month-long emphasis accentuated by weekly sermons and a few banquets. The food part was yummy, but preaching four consecutive sermons on biblical stewardship had me worried as to my job security.

Any student of Scripture will understand that God often acts only in response to faith. In our case it became clear that God was waiting to see if we were serious in our pursuit of His leading us to relocate because within a month following the campaign launch God opened a door that had been previously closed and we purchased a large piece of property within walking distance of our existing campus. I must add that we were able to purchase it for a third of the going price per acre we had been encountering in our search the previous nine months.

It would be around this time that God opened our eyes to an ongoing church-wide study called *Crown Financial*. A study developed by Larry Burkett. We organized and invited members to take this 13 week long study on biblical stewardship. This study would be offered one to three times a year for the next ten years. After that we changed to Dave Ramsey's *Financial Peace University* making it available at least twice a year since. As you can see we are far removed from fearing the subject of stewardship to discovering the enormous blessings that God brings upon His people, their families and His church when we practice biblical stewardship.

I mentioned a moment ago that the stewardship campaign we entered into was but the first of two. While that first campaign enabled us to purchase that nice piece of land and have a nest egg for the future build, it was not enough. While our best laid plans can get derailed, such was the case when the loan we thought we would get at the end of that campaign fell through. Needless-to-say, our only recourse was to launch a second campaign. I need to repeat myself here and state that these decisions are made by the church family. Given the fact they unanimously agreed is evidence of God's leading and the consequence of His people learning biblical stewardship.

Again, I worried that I would still have a job after preaching four consecutive sermons on stewardship and a capital campaign. You might appreciate what I am saying better if you understood that this second campaign was launched the Sunday right after the tragedy of 9/11. While the campaign leader and I were not sure we should launch it we both agreed with our President that we cannot let terrorists keep us from pursuing what we deem best. Incredibly we raised a third more in that campaign than in the previous one which put us in a position to build the first phase of construction.

What happens when the church learns biblical stewardship? Remarkable things happen. I will say more about this in the ensuing chapters but suffice it to say, teach and preach stewardship. Lives will be changed, marriages will be restored, missions will be funded, staff will be added and more souls will be reached. I could go on but you get the idea.

So, what if your church learns biblical stewardship? Brace yourself when they do because the doors of ministry are about to fly wide open. Let me encourage you to be the facilitator of your church learning biblical stewardship and raise up others to help you equip the saints with the life changing truths of biblical stewardship.

What if...your treasurer embezzles money?

Sometimes our Christian sensitivities get the better of us. I am talking about the desire to trust those who profess allegiance to Jesus to the degree we allow them access to funds without any considerable oversight. Not to suggest we hold all those who handle church funds as suspect, we are wise to take note that Jesus did have his issues with a treasurer.

One of the things about doing business/ministry in the church is that we need to have an accountability to one another. Regardless the position there must be some identifiable, proactive means of insuring we are helping each other avoid the tempter's snare. Holding "one another" accountable for godly behavior and holy living is at the core of being in fellowship with other believers as the church family. We need each other to walk the straight and narrow. We need each other to help us chose to do right and strive to let everything we do honor Christ. This accountability is equally important in helping each other do ministry.

When it comes to the ministry of stewardship and management of our funds our situation was not anything out of the norm in that we did have a stewardship committee who looked over the finances periodically. At the time of the embezzlement we had a stewardship committee that consisted of corporate financial officers, bankers and even an IRS agent. We did have what may be considered normal and expected protocols in place but apparently they were not enough. With hindsight being 20/20 we discovered some system flaws that allowed our treasurer to embezzle a considerable amount of money over a two year period.

This all came to light as we were nearing the end of the 3rd year of our second capital stewardship campaign when our treasurer became very ill and we had to have a stewardship team member step in to do the books. It was then we discovered that nearly $130,000 was missing from our building fund. I'll not go into details as to how the treasurer was able to do this. Just suffice it to say, we put a much better system in place with steps to greatly minimize any opportunity for mismanagement and to protect those who handle our funds from any discrimination.

For you nerd types (Dave Ramsey's identifier) our treasurer can no longer sign a check. They do not have access to the bank accounts except to look at registries and balances. There are monthly meetings with the stewardship committee and treasurer along with an intermittent one-on-one between the treasurer and the chair of that committee. The lines of communication are much more aggressive and clearer.

As it turns out important information was withheld from us when vetting the treasurer who committed this fraud and in time their dubious history caught up with them resulting in prison time. Sad outcome and not what we were looking for, especially when it comes to God's command to forgive. They had two young children and a spouse who was stationed at our nearby Army post, Fort Huachuca. It is grievous how they forfeited those relationships because they could not be content with what God was providing for them.

One may wonder as to what keeps a church from imploding from such a significant loss. After all we were working hard at growing our building fund to the point where we could begin the process of relocation. I will admit that more than once I asked God why He let that happen. We could simply conclude that it was our fault for having a less than adequate system of checks and balances which could then be taken advantage of by a quasi-Judas. And yet we ultimately have to wonder why God would direct us to take on the herculean task of buying land, raising funds, hiring architects and contractors all at great expense. You may be surprised at what God told me; and has reminded me on numerous occasions; the money is His and He can do with it as He pleases.

In our instance, God allowed this theft to take place in order to teach us some important lessons. Lessons like the need to have our accounting system multilayered, to be challenged to forgive and to learn, yet again, what it means to trust God.

We needed to see our accounting vulnerability because down the road we would be in possession of significantly more funds than those embezzled (that is coming up in a future chapter). God also needed to teach us that forgiveness is required, even if it is embezzlement. And God needed to teach us to trust Him. To trust in His ability to replenish that $130,000 many times over. Which, by the way, He has, in fact, done over time. Had we given in to the fleshly desire for retribution seeking a pound of flesh and thus refusing to trust in God's providence and sovereignty; I have absolutely no doubt that He would have simply removed our lamp stand.

So, what if your treasurer embezzles money? Hopefully you will never have to experience that, but if you should, practice grace and forgiveness but let the law hold them accountable. The best response you can give to this story is for you to proactively put into place the kind of precautionary steps that will remove the prospects of embezzlement ever happening.

What if... you have conflict with a church staff member?

I realize that many of the pastors reading this are not in a setting where you have paid full-time staff. I qualify them as "full-time" for the purpose of highlighting the increased level of difficulty that comes when they are creating problems for the team and you cannot just invite them to quit. Whether single or married, they need an income to provide for themselves and their family a sense of stability and security.

I fully recognize that there are different types of pastors and that some of you reading this do not have a problem designing an immediate exit strategy for the problem staff member. I am just not one of those. I will admit that I default on the longsuffering side of the equation in that I will try any number of things to address the problem before I strongly encourage them to leave. I want you to understand that in the mix is my clumsy way of seeking resolution. I put it that way because I have had to learn by trial and error. Because I dislike confrontation I will look for any number of solutions that are more equitable than "you're fired!"

While I appreciate every staff member I have worked with sometimes a difference of philosophy is discovered and makes it very difficult to move forward in a unified way. It is pretty clear that the Scriptures teach us the absolute necessity of unity being what identifies the church family. Notwithstanding, there will always be times of disagreement simply because we are individuals and not clones. But with respect to the heavy responsibility of the senior or lead pastor to give direction to the church as best he understands it, it is incumbent upon those who follow his leadership to be doing the things necessary to help and not hinder that. And the closer the working relationship the greater the need to work together and not against one another.

One of the particular hurdles that I have had to deal with is my underestimating God's ability to make His Bride resilient. That when a staff member is needing to move on the church will survive. I have prolonged the inevitable too many times out of a fear for some fall-out causing irreparable harm to the church. The bottom line is that none of us are indispensable. I know, that is a depressing thought, but it is true!

If the church suffers significant loss of membership because a lead or staff pastor moves on then it has been nothing more than a house of cards, not a church pursuing a New Testament model. Of course we all want people to like us. And, there are those who develop an affinity to certain leaders and will be saddened by their departure. Again, nothing wrong with that. But to become angry and leave the church is nothing more than highlighting a spiritual immaturity that comes from a lack of understanding regarding the purpose of the church.

One of the keys to the ability for our church to withstand the potential for a fallout from a staff dismissal is our strong emphasis on the need for each member to be invested in a small group. Our small groups meet on campus Sunday mornings or in homes during the week. In some instances the small group is defined by one's involvement with a particular ministry. Small groups are where genuine relationships are established and are the tie that binds more than any other aspect of church life including the fidelity one may have to a staff member.

I have had to come to grips with the reality that the church belongs to Jesus and to fear people getting upset and leaving over staff dismissal is a fear that does not come from God. Incidentally, a similar fear haunted me with the prospects of people fleeing in the aftermath of the four consecutive stewardship messages I needed to deliver to launch each capital stewardship campaign. Also in the mix is my fear of people seeking my down fall. Such a fear is a combination of paranoia and a lack of faith with a little theological negligence thrown in. We all react to conflict in different ways. Some strike back by going on the offensive clashing sabers with their detractors. Still others will shrink back into a feeling of despair and wonder if they should move on. You may not like this, but at the heart of most of our reactions is pride. We think we need to defend our integrity by either taking them out at the knees or quitting as if to protect our dignity. It is pride.

I have been blessed to have been surrounded by some pretty incredible staff members. The kind that make you look good even when you do not deserve it. But there have been a couple of staff over the years who have presented me with some significant challenges. On one occasion the staff member was attempting to gather around themselves persons sympathetic to their agenda and create a veritable coup against me. Despite my lengthy efforts to reason with him through mediation he remained unrepentant. At the time I sought advice from a trusted source who said very simply, "Let God defend you. If you are sincerely seeking the face of God and humbly striving to serve Him, then let Him defend you." I have found that piece of advice indispensable and credit it for my privilege of being in one place for such a long time.

Another source of encouragement is found in the writings of the fifteenth century Puritan, Richard Baxter, who challenged his parishioners to understand that when they choose God's glory for their purpose they would never need to fear.

I will not mislead you by making it sound easy. It takes faith and patience to trust God to defend you and He does so by His Spirit. None of the earth opening and swallowing folks as in the days of Moses. God simply brings a person under conviction or He orchestrates events that expose the true nature of their heart. All I know is that God is faithful to complete the work to which He has called us. It is critical during this time of trust and patience we do not wrestle the steering wheel away from the Holy Spirit. I can only imagine how this vital truth could have enabled many pastors to stay the course at a given ministry station had they known it.

Conflict is inevitable. I have learned not to avoid it or exacerbate it by overreacting. Communicate all the time. Pray together. Hold one another accountable. Speak the truth in love. Seek wise counsel. And most importantly, love and forgive others the same way Christ loves and forgives you. When you have pursued all that, let God defend you and take the steps necessary to lead the church without fearing her collapse.

So, what if you have conflict with a church staff member? What steps are you taking to resolve that conflict? And, more importantly, are those steps in accordance with Scripture?

What if... the church buys property in your absence?

This may not mean much to some, but to this pastor whose goal is to lead a congregation who seeks God's will for themselves, it is spectacular.

The backstory is that shortly after the first capital stewardship campaign to raise funds to purchase land we were still not certain where God would have us relocate. We had a property search team busily looking at various commercial properties in the area, but nothing was feeling right. Either it was a chunk of land that could only be partially used for development or the person seeking to sell it, let us say, had a less than desirable reputation. We had been steadily looking for nine months to no avail. It was time for a vacation, least for Nancy, me and our children.

Interestingly, up to this point in time in my pastoral career I had never thought it a good idea to be gone more than a week at a time. Somewhere along the way I was led to believe that things could come undone if the shepherd is gone too long. What a bunch of caca. I had finally matured enough to recognize two things. If my leadership had any depth and value the church leaders could handle my being gone more than a week. And, secondly, it takes more than a week to just unwind and begin to relax!

So I took the plunge and made plans for a two week vacation. By the way, Pastor, plan it so you are not having to preach a sermon right after you get back. No rest on vacation when you have to put in the hours necessary for sermon prep. Anyway, we took off to a cabin in New Mexico that Nancy's family owned. We thoroughly enjoyed ourselves. What made it particularly exciting was to come home to some incredible news—our trustees had signed a contract on a piece of property within walking distance of our current campus!

God can work in some very interesting ways and this was certainly one of them. It was probably a few months prior that I had sat down in the home of some dear friends from my days at First Baptist and asked them if they were aware of any land for sale in the area. He had been one of the principle land owners and developers of Sierra Vista as far back as the late 1950's. It so happened they were attempting to sell the fifty acres they were sitting on in order to move to Tucson and be closer to the medical services they needed there. While I was not visiting them to make an appeal to buy some of their acreage, they wanted me to know they wished they could sell us a portion of their property but needed to sell their whole plot in order to make it more marketable. Of course, I respected that and did not think anything more of it.

Apparently, they had a change of heart and contacted a principle member of our land search team and proposed selling us 37 of the 50 acres. That information was conveyed to the necessary parties within the church leadership and, having received the approval of the congregation to act on their behalf, the deal was sealed.

What excited me about all of this is how the church did not need my approval. Nor did they feel they had to have it before the decision could be made. I was unaware of the purchase until I returned home. What a remarkable and wonderful surprise. To the less than confident pastor the feeling may not have been elation but fear. Fear that they had somehow lost "control." Every wise shepherd knows you do not "control" sheep, you lead them. What the decision to act in my absence told me is that I was on the right track in my leadership. That everything was in place for such a decision to be made, even in my absence.

Understand that what is going on here is not some back room, let us see what we can get away with, deal. It is a result of clear communication between the leadership and congregation. We had been communicating all along either through business meetings or town hall meetings (informational in nature) and letting everyone have a hand in the process. The congregation, as a whole, had voted to give the land search committee the authority to act on their behalf. And yes, a modicum of trust had to be in place for that to happen. But trust is what is generated when you have open, honest and forthright conversations. It is the behind the back whispers that ensures mistrust.

Some may wonder if I am advocating some kind of reckless independence on the part of the membership. Nothing could be further from the truth. What is in view is not about independence, but dependence. Dependency upon one another in the decision making process. Of depending on the efforts put forth to act when God's will is presented and not have to have all kinds of meetings before one can act. This is about preparing the soil for the planting. Not tiling it after the seed has been dropped.

Granted, there are some decisions that do not and should not require the "congregation" to approve. But when it comes to buying land and relocating then all hands on deck is the watchword. Communicate clearly and often and you will have prepared the soil of decision making to happen even if you are not present.

So, what if the church buys property in your absence? Rejoice! You are leading well!

What if... what you have been taught is not working?

What I have in mind here are some of the things I was taught in seminary and also learned as an observant church member. Specifically, I am talking about the way the church does business in the gathering referred to as "the business meeting."

While earning my Master's degree in Religious Education much effort was put into the area of church administration and within that the proper way to run a business meeting. Especially in the use of the Robert's Rules of Order. These rules of order emerged during the American industrial age as a good way to get business done in an orderly and efficient way. That part of it appealed to me but as I became engaged in the process as a church leader it became apparent to me that while efficient and orderly we were a church and not a business. We were members of a living, loving body of believers and not shareholders and business men and women.

Of particular interest was how the Roberts Rules of Order was intended to manage people's input. Even quash that input if it did not get a second. Even that does not always work. Cannot tell you how many times someone would second a motion not because they were interested or saw value to the motion, but that they were merely curious. Boy has that allowed a can of worms to be opened many a time.

Another inherent problem with this business model is that it also allows a few to ramrod or hijack an otherwise peaceful discussion. There seems to be in every church those who seek to stand on their own platform with which to prove how much they know and the congregation does not. I know, I am a preacher saying this and I have such a platform every week! Hopefully, my attitude is not to beat my chest or make everyone feel out of step but to show the love of God through the Scriptures.

The real conundrum for me was how we could launch into a godly, spirit-filled business meeting and suddenly see it deteriorate into disagreement and posturing. By-the-way, these kinds of experiences in my pastorate have almost all been exclusively during a budget adoption business meeting. I suspect Jesus had such a meeting in mind when he said, *"The love of money is the root of all evil"* (1st Timothy 6:10). Thankfully, our budget adoption meetings were only once a year and suffering with the less than godly opining was limited to that. Even so, I could not find rest in my pastoral soul with just that. Ultimately, what I was taught and influenced by for nearly four decades proved to be a model that lent itself to being unhealthy at times. Eventually this led me to fast and pray. I knew there had to be a better way and I would only find it in the counsel of God's Word.

That set me upon a journey that involved an in-depth study of all the places in the New Testament where the church gathered to do business. It also involved my reading resources outside the regular diet of SBC articles. What I found was a variety of ways to carry out the business of the church in ways that do not open the door for dissension while opening other doors for more fruitful conversation.

What was arrived at was a document I hammered out after numerous conversations with fellow staff followed with a presentation to our Church Council. Once I had their approval it was presented to the congregation. They were given a month to consider the proposition and when we next convened in a business session it would be the last such meeting under Roberts Rules of Order. What the congregation embraced was now called *Biblical Rules of Order*. I know, not very creative on my part, but it does clarify what we want to be our guiding rule. You will find this document in Appendix I.

For those of you who may be curious to know, the way we approach the whole financial and budget conversation is very different now. Ultimately, we want to give members an opportunity to address their concerns on the financial front but to do so in the company of those who can address them more efficiently than in a business meeting setting. Our budget process begins with the various ministry leaders and staff submitting their budget requests to the Stewardship Committee who then studies them. If there is need to discuss the submittal a meeting is arranged. Once the budget has been put together it then goes out to the congregation who are given a two week time frame to look it over and contact either the ministry leader of the budget line they are concerned about, the Stewardship team or the Treasurer. If a member has a question that is best addressed before the entire Stewardship committee a meeting is arranged. Consequently, everyone is given a chance to inquire and discuss any aspect of the budget prior to its adoption.

After the two week review the budget is then presented either as is or amended according to any changes that may have occurred. If there are changes they are typically an accounting correction. Any major changes to the budget involves extending the time line so that the congregation can review those changes. In the ten years we have been following this process the congregation has had whatever questions or concerns they had regarding the budget answered prior to sitting in a business session. The wonderful outcome is the absence of those uncomfortable and negative business meetings to which we were subjected.

One of the challenges a pastor can expect when pursuing this manner of business is that when the budget comes up for adoption there is no discussion. That has already been done. I have found it healthy and helpful for the Stewardship chair to say a word about the budget and the excitement of what God is doing through our church. After this, all the pastor need do is ask for the congregation's approval. Whether it is the budget in question or some other item for approval I preface it with the question, "Do you believe it is God's will for Village Meadows that we…?" Admittedly it gets a little mystical for me at this point because all I am looking for is a robust "amen." Sometimes it is not as robust as I want because I have asked for an opinion that involves the question of God's will. The heightened level of seriousness tends to make a person hesitate. Nothing wrong with that when you are asking your people to be discerning about God's will for the church.

Because I am looking for an obvious consensus from the congregation, I have to be prepared to postpone the decision if it appears there is not a clear majority. That has yet to happen and that may be due to the level of communication and opportunity for ownership we give the congregation before we bring the recommendation before them. Incidentally, we do not call for the *yes* and *no* vote with a show of hands. That only serves to revert us back to a time when a select few wanted to usurp the Spirit is moving. We will, however, ask for a ballot vote when hiring full-time pastoral staff.

Another outcome of this shift to biblical rules of order is that we now call our business meetings "Ministry Celebrations." Since there is not always "business" to take care of why not celebrate what God has been doing! You can also do that with the business being addressed. It has been interesting to see how this has evolved. The important thing is to keep it interesting and not sound like a monotonous reading of data. You know, like a business report.

Over time the church has decided to have Ministry Celebrations (business meetings) twice a year. In April and November. The one in November is to approve the budget and affirm the ministry volunteers for the coming year. Most of our time is spent recognizing and thanking those who have served the previous year.

While we may only have two Ministry Celebrations a year there is always the ability to have "special called" business meetings should the need arise. When it comes to needing to inform the congregation and even have a public conversation with no official approval to be asked for we will have a Town Hall Meeting.

When what you have been taught is not working; at least not to godly standards; prayerfully go to God's Word and see if He has a better idea.

So, what if what you have been taught is not working? Pray with an open mind to be able to hear and see how the Holy Spirit will lead you through Scripture to that which will work.

What if... you do not have enough room for your small group ministry?

Some may wonder why, in the face of so many challenges before today's church, that this should be of enough concern to be addressed in this book. The answer is a biblical one. In particular are the core values of the biblical church which has within them the essential need for small groups.

One of the first classes I took in seminary back in 1976, was on group dynamics. I almost laughed out loud when the professor informed us that after decades of research in the area of group dynamics the experts had determined that the optimum size of a group in which interpersonal, meaningful interaction can take place is…wait for it…twelve! It occurred to me that the King of all creation had already established that number two millennia prior.

While one may want to have the support of scientific findings, our trust in how Jesus went about organizing his church ought to be enough. He chose twelve because he knows his creation and the prime environment in which to learn from one another. While it is suggested that rabbi's in Jesus' day chose twelve disciples to match the number of tribes in Israel, our Lord's aim was disciple making and not merely keeping with tradition. Jesus was going to establish his church around small groups, and his plans have not changed.

Years ago I read that the larger you grow in number as a congregation the smaller you must become. That advice had to do with small groups. The more souls God adds to your church family the more small groups you need to create. From a purely church growth perspective, when you add small groups you correspondently grow. The challenge is to find and train leaders from which to establish these new groups.

Our journey at Village Meadows has been to do just that, although it is a significant challenge given the transient nature of our particular demographic (military town). Not long after I arrived as pastor and began to lead an already growing congregation we set about trying to create new small groups which we called Sunday school classes back then. It was not long before we were faced with the challenge of finding places to put them. Again, as we created more small groups the congregation grew. It was at this time we had to become creative as well as have a paradigm shift.

When it comes to the traditional Southern Baptist Church the thinking then was that we had to have our small groups all meet on campus and on Sunday mornings. Hence, "Sunday school." There are obvious plusses to having small groups on Sunday morning at the church. It is then you have other age group ministries organized to disciple children at the same time their parents are engaged in a small group. Because we had run out of room at our campus we were forced to think outside the box and had to look for space off campus. It was a bitter sweet time. Sweet in that we were growing; bitter in that we had to go to some less than "churchy" locations.

Fortunately for us we had an elementary school just across the street and were able to use/rent classroom space. Principally the children and youth met there. Had something to do with posteriors and chair size. Our adult small groups met in nearby homes as well as the local funeral home (the mortician was a member of our church). We were doing whatever it took to make disciples which meant that we had to accommodate our growing small group ministry in off-campus sites. It helped that we had decided to relocate and by now had purchased the land nearby.

When it came time to decide what to build first on the new site we concluded that since we were enjoying a beautiful and relatively new sanctuary at our current campus our greater need was small group space. For me personally I had my concerns as to this choice, but God affirmed in my heart that this was the right thing to do. Of course it was the right choice because the small group discipleship ministry is at the center of what it means to be a New Testament church.

An important piece of knowledge to have in this conversation is how most of the New Testament epistles were written to believers in specific communities who met primarily in house churches. Given the architecture of the day, most all of those house churches could only accommodate a group of twelve plus their children. Regarding our Sunday gatherings the modern day church is an anomaly when compared to the first century church. They met almost exclusively in small groups. This becomes particularly poignant when reading the many passages that address how we are to relate to and treat "one another." It is important to recognize that building relationships according to Scripture is something you cannot do while sitting in a worship service which is biblically designed to have a primary interaction with one—God. Furthermore, the worship service is certainly not about meeting one's needs except the need to worship God in Spirit and in truth (John 4:24).

Granted there are those few churches who grow numerically on the basis of contemporary music and good preaching but offer no small group ministry. Of interest is how we will have believers from those churches consider ours because they long for interpersonal relationships. This speaks to the fundamental need we all have to be in relationships with others. Which brings me to point out again the presence of the "one another" relational passages throughout the New Testament. See Appendix II for a sample list of the "one another's." Incidentally, our music is blended and good. I will leave someone else to write about the quality of the preaching.

As time has passed and we have understood the need to keep adding small groups God has been good to bring us leaders who have been skilled in the organization of home small groups that meet other than Sunday mornings. These home small groups offer a different dynamic in that they are in a setting that feels less institutional and do not have as much of the time constraints as Sunday morning schedules. They also enjoy a closer family environment in that they share a meal with all ages. The one significant challenge is the child care needed while they meet for Bible study and adult interaction.

The point to all of this effort at making small groups a priority is that it is critical to the maturing of believers. It is the most crucial way of teaching the biblical truths of what it means to live within the faith community and the necessity of being accountable to one another. It is also the biblical model for how we care for one another; and how each believer in their respective small group is to minister to one another. We're not leaving that responsibility to a select few like a pastor or deacon. They have their purpose but it is not to do what we are "all" called to be and do which is to care one for another (see Ephesians 4:11-16).

Not only are we to care for one another we are to admonish or hold one another accountable (see Colossians 3:16). What most fail to recognize is that when you find church discipline in the New Testament it is principally taking place in the Small Group. I have had some come to me over the years and want to know if we practice church discipline. In their mind the evidence of such a practice is in the public humiliation of an unrepentant member. Naturally, only after we have properly applied the instructions laid out in Matthew 18.

Two problems are at hand here. Someone wants to be satisfied you are not avoiding church discipline which is to say they are not happy with you until you prove it to them. That is nothing shy of an ungodly attitude. Secondly, the expectation is that the wayward member is paraded in front of the congregation to face their sin. I have been told such an action will warn others to watch their steps and avoid similar moral failure. The same thing was once said about public executions.

While I do not want to get caught up in a debate about capital punishment, I do want us to consider the biblical model of how small groups are where church discipline is to occur. And it is to occur through the counsel of 1st Corinthians 13 which is within the same letter a small group in Corinth was being instructed to discipline a member who was living in unrepentant sin. They were to lovingly call him to repentance and if refused to lovingly remove him from their fellowship; from their small group. Later on a second letter instructed them on how to lovingly bring him back into their small group.

Incidentally, our small groups are not about seeing how much more knowledge we can gain. That only leads to pridefulness (1st Corinthians 8:1). Our aim is to apply the truths of Scripture and in that to mature in our knowledge and understanding.

As much as my own pride wants to believe that the growth of a disciple rests on my preaching, well, it takes a back seat to the importance of having each believer experiencing the unique dynamic of a small group around which Christ established and organized his church.

So, what if you do not have enough room for your small group ministry? Pray and work with your leadership to do more than discuss the problem but establish specific steps to take. The making of disciples is at stake!

What if... you go against tradition? (Part I)

You are probably thinking this will be a chapter on music styles. Sorry to disappoint you, but it is about the traditional model or way of thinking we commonly have about the role of the pastor. Given the New Testament's general teaching on the role of the pastor as the one who leads and feeds the flock it is easy to see how he can be held in high regard. As far as the calling and position are concerned that is indeed the proper way to see one's pastor. However, this tendency to elevate the pastor has also lent itself to seeing him also as one who is the "professional;" the "minister" of the church. By implication, he and all other vocational "minister's" are to do the work of ministry and the members are to support them in that work. This traditional view of the pastoral leadership is a grave misunderstanding and unbiblical.

To believe that the pastor is to be "the minister" to the needs of the flock and ultimately to the community at large is not scriptural. Understandably, this model works, although weakly, in the smaller church with an average attendance of 80 or less, which make up the majority of churches in America. That is because a pastor can manage the care for a small congregation and perpetuate the idea that he is the only one sufficiently trained to be the primary minister.

I believe this idea of the pastor as "the minister" probably found its start in the development of Catholicism with its hierarchical system of authority relegating the laity to be merely receivers only of the "ministry" of the ordained. While Martin Luther tried to break this mold by placing the Scriptures into the hands of the general population of believers, the tendency to continue to see the pastoral role as significantly superior to all others in the church still remained, thus a continuation of the false perception that "ministry" is done by the ordained.

For clarification, the *ministry* I am speaking of here has to do with the decision of whether or not a member is satisfied that they have been ministered to when in need. It is the attitude that concludes a person has not "really been ministered to" unless the pastor (in some larger churches, the Senior Pastor) has visited them. That can also be said of the deacons. That is to say, if there is a need then notify the pastor or the deacons since they are the ones "set apart" to do *ministry.*

This is where a grave error is made and one I believe has woefully minimized the effectiveness of the average New Testament church. If ministry does not happen—if Jesus cannot touch a life unless it is through the efforts of an official clergyman of the church—then we will always see pastors "burn-out" which is something that has been happening at alarming rates in America for the past 40 years.

The biblical model for ministry is concisely and comprehensively given in Ephesians 4:11-16 which I want you to stop and read right now (imagine music playing in the background with this pause).

"And he himself gave some to be apostles, some prophets, some evangelists, some pastors and teachers, equipping the saints for the work of ministry, to build up the body of Christ, until we all reach unity in the faith and in the knowledge of God's Son, growing into maturity with a stature measured by Christ's fullness. Then we will no longer be little children, tossed by the waves and blown around by every wind of teaching, by human cunning with cleverness in the techniques of deceit. But speaking the truth in love, let us grow in every way into him who is the head—Christ. From him the whole body, fitted and knit together by every supporting ligament, promotes the growth of the body for building up itself in love by the proper working of each individual part." (Ephesians 4:11–16, CSB)

As you just read, the primary role of those whom Christ gave/ordained/appointed to give leadership to the church do so by training the saints (the laity) to <u>do</u> the work of "ministry." What a powerful text; one that empowers every member of the church body to be qualified to represent Christ in ministering to others. When coupled with the passages that teach us of our personal spiritual gift-mix with which we each edify the church (Romans 12:3-8; 1st Corinthians 12), it should be crystal clear that the **ministry to the church is by the church** and not relegated to just a select few. Add to this Peter's admonition in 1st Peter 4:10, *"Based on the gift they have received, everyone should use it to serve others, as good managers of the varied grace of God."*

Let me pause here and make sure I am not being misunderstood. I am not looking for a way out of making visits, counseling, intervening in crises or avoiding other ministry opportunities. I understand that there are those moments when a member is nearing death's door or is in the throes of a devastating crisis that a visit from the Pastor offers a unique blessing. Add to this the fact that I love to be with God's people. I love to visit; to minister as God has gifted me, and to contribute what I can from my education and experience. But not as a hired hand. Ministry to the church is to be by the church (Ephesians 4:12). And it is when we ALL minister that the church is made whole as we are shown in the Ephesians 4 passage.

A significant truth found in the New Testament epistles is the necessity of each member to be doing ministry according to the spiritual gifts God has given them. The pastor/teacher is to equip them in the use of those gifts which then leads to the building up of the Body of Christ through their individual ministry.

With this understanding of God's Word I am free to be an obedient steward of my time as the "pastor." The Greek word from which the word pastor is derived is *poimen* and is literally translated, "the one who feeds." That means I must be devoting the majority of my time in prayer and preparation. A good example of this is seen in Acts 6. To fail at prayer and preparation is to literally fail at all other points of being a shepherd to God's people.

Two things have occurred in my life that have motivated me to look long and hard at this matter. They are shepherding a church for spiritual growth and a being a godly husband to a chronically ill wife.

When I first came to Village Meadows it was me and one full-time secretary. As our church grew the ability to continue in a traditional pastoral methodology of being "the minister" became increasingly problematic. Then my wife Nancy's illness pressed me to make changes that in reality are more in step with Scripture. Certainly putting my family first before the church is critical and no one who is biblically literate would argue that. Even so, there was a great deal of pressure flowing against the tide of tradition when my ability to be away from the house for the "expected appearances" of the pastor had to be reduced to the true essentials. I have only been able to do this because of the gracious spirit of the Village Meadows family who have embraced the truths of Ephesian 4. And, had that grace and compassion not been offered, sadly I would not have been able to continue as pastor there, much less anywhere.

Unless we grasp the truth that the ministry of the church is to be by the church there will always be members whose needs are not being met and just as many more who are not enjoying the ministry God intends for them through the use of their spiritual gifts.

So, what if you go against tradition? Expect some push back. However, if you communicate your intentions well through careful Bible instruction you might just successfully win out over tradition. A sobering, but timely passage at this juncture, would be Mark 7:13 where Jesus confronts the misguided traditions of the Pharisees by saying, *"You nullify the word of God by your traditions that you have handed down. And you do many other similar things."*

What if...you go against tradition? (Part II)

As I have discerned my role as pastor with regards to "ministry" I have also been compelled to let this discernment impact those who are assigned in Scripture to serve along side of me—our deacons. While our desire is that the deacon ministry be modeled after the New Testament church we are not given a whole lot of information with which to understand that model. Because of this we are left to speculate to some degree, which, of course, opens the door to the potential of a misguided interpretation or should I say extrapolation. It is from here I move prayerfully and cautiously. For some of you, what you are about to read may flow against the traditions you are familiar with regarding the deacon ministry.

Given the scriptural teaching that the "ministry to the church is by the church" we are confronted with a traditional role of a deacon. In that traditional role among Southern Baptists the deacon has been a part of *The Deacon Family Ministry Plan; The Deacon Team Ministry Plan* or some other forms in between. In most of these plans the deacon is serving the needs of the body in one capacity or another. While a noble endeavor I do not believe it captures the true meaning and duty of the New Testament deacon. Furthermore, it perpetuates the philosophy of a select few being the ministers.

As one searches the Scriptures for the use and meaning of the Greek word *diakonos*, from which we derive our English word for *deacon*, it is important to understand that the word is used to describe a person who runs errands or executes the commands of another. In other words, they serve at the pleasure of another.

Even with its singular meaning it is interesting to see how the word *diakonos* has a dual application in the New Testament. In its broadest sense the word identifies "anyone" who is serving in any capacity (see Romans 13:4 and 6; 15:8, 16:1). Then you have it describing the *office* of a "deacon." A good example of this contrast is between 1st Timothy 3:8-13 and 4:6.

We are first introduced to the concept of the office of a *deacon* in Acts 6:1-6 where seven men were set apart—ordained—to serve the physical needs of the church freeing the pastors to focus on the study of the Word and prayer. However, since the word *diakonos* is not used in the Acts 6 narrative you have to conclude that these seven men were the charter members of the *office* of a deacon later introduced in 1st Timothy 3:8-13. The assumption that Acts 6 introduces us to the first deacons is made on the basis of their call to "serve" the needs of the people thus connecting it to the idea of *diakonos* used in 1st Timothy 3.

Because we have only Acts 6 as a model for the "function" of a deacon we are vulnerable to misinterpreting and thus misapplying what that function should be. This is why it is of utmost importance to let the only concise description of the deacon qualifications in 1st Timothy 3 serve as our key text from which we try to determine the deacon's biblical role in the church.

The only two places *diakonos* is used as a proper noun is in Paul's salutation in Philippians 1:1 and then in 1st Timothy 3:8-13. Assuming that the seven men described in Acts 6 were in fact the first deacons serving in a specific capacity (serving food to Greek widows) when we move forward some 30 to 40 years to Paul's first letter to Timothy it becomes clear that the criteria for being a deacon had become more stringent. It had moved from men in Acts 6 having a *"good reputation"* to additional stipulations in 1st Timothy 3. Therefore, the office of a deacon had an obvious maturing process that it went through in the early church.

The question that remains is what more, if any, did the responsibility of this office exceed that which we can deduce from Acts 6. In other words, is today's deacon to be defined by more than one who serves the needs of the body in order to free up the pastor(s) for prayer and preparation?

To answer this question we must do three things:

- First, maintain the understanding that "ministry" or "serving" is something all the saints are to be doing.

- Second, begin to understand the activity in Acts 6 not as much a service rendered to the church (the serving of the Greek widows) but more as a service rendered to the apostles (pastors). They were freeing the apostles from that responsibility thus meeting their need to spend their time in prayer and preparation. The truth of the matter is that these first deacons were more *peacemakers* than waiters.

- Thirdly, we must look seriously at the extensiveness of the conditions laid out for service as a deacon in 1st Timothy 3. Those conditions take on what I see as a "righteous" or "holy" delineation. In comparison to the requirements of the pastor in 1st Timothy 3:1-7 there is little difference in the qualifications save the pastor is to have the gift of teaching.

I have concluded that these high and holy standards have something to do with the need to ensure that those who felt God's calling to be deacons (and pastors) were men who understood what it meant to be a humble servant of Christ; who strove to be filled with the Holy Spirit, readily confessing their sins and striving to be at peace with others. I believe these stipulations have more to do with the *private* life of the man being called as opposed to his *public* life; that he is first and foremost a humble, spirit-filled follower of Christ in his heart which finds its evidence in his lifestyle.

Matthew 20:20-28 and Mark 10:35-45 contain the record of Christ's insistence that the true role of a disciple is to be a servant to everyone else. This lesson came in the midst of some of his closest disciples arguing over who was going to hold positions of prominence/leadership in His pending kingdom. It makes sense to me then that this criterion for the *diakonos* reflects the precise attitude Jesus was identifying.

To be set apart (ordained) by your peers is a high honor; one which could all too easily go to the head of a man who does not understand the true meaning of that honor. There is no question the need for humility is of utmost importance and consistently represented in the overall theme of 1st Timothy. Therefore, it is my contention that when attempting to discern what the deacon's role is to be, you have to interpret it through Christ's description of the humble servant. As such those churches where the deacons become ruling boards or authoritative administrators have missed the whole point of the Scriptures teaching on the *diakonos*.

The deacons I am privileged to serve with are men whom I look to for wise counsel. They are men, who along with their wives, I can count on to work hard to ensure the unity of the church. Who will defend the truth of God's Word without hesitation and constantly be in intercessory prayer for their pastor and his family. I do not come up with things for them to do. Rather, I expect them to simply be deacons—men who serve their pastor and seek the welfare of the church family.

So, what if you go against the traditional model of deacon ministry in your church? You might be surprised that when equipping the saints to do ministry your deacons are free to assist you in spiritual and pastoral ways you never imagined.

[Further thoughts on the deacon and pastoral roles can be found in Appendix III.]

I believe that the pathway to having exceptional leaders in your church is what I call "The Ephesians 4 Factor." That is the passage I shared with you in a previous chapter. It is through a comprehensive understanding of the *equipping the saints for work of ministry* you discover that when believers are being discipled/equipped that leaders will emerge. Not just any kind of leader, but exceptional godly leaders. It should not be a surprise that leaders are a natural outcome of believers being taught how to apply the truths of Scripture. And when leaders are raised up the body of Christ is built up.

One of the major challenges that a pastor faces is how to disciple the church family at large. At the very least the pastor is hopeful that if he exegetes a passage well and then preaches it in clear ways it will result in believers growing in their faith. One would hope so. However, it is going to fall terribly short if that is all the pastor is banking on to make disciples out of his congregants.

It is my humble opinion that the modern day worship service as a whole is intended for the worshiper to express their love to God through corporate singing and prayer. Then, in that posture of worship, to listen carefully for God to speak to them through the sermon. A worship service is the unique opportunity to experience and fortify one's faith in God through their encounter with God. It is not, however, the most substantive way of equipping the saints.

Keep in mind that the New Testament was written and delivered principally to small groups. So, when you read pivotal passages like we find in Ephesians 4 the context in which they are carried out is that of a small group. Try to imagine how the pastor/teacher would implement the equipping of the saints. There would be singing and praying and preaching. But there would also be dialogue in the midst of instruction. There would have been the same dynamic we strive for at Village Meadows in our small groups which is to learn how to be doers of the Word and not listeners only (James 1:22).

When it comes to a congregation that is larger than 12 adults the need for additional small groups is in order. Also, the pastor's equipping ministry must become more individualized. Instead of attempting to "equip the saints" through sermons he must equip the small group leaders to be able to equip small group members.

Over the years I have read and been told how one-on-one discipleship is essential if believers are going to mature as disciples. Even though I knew this was good advice I could not figure out how I could personally do that efficiently for each member. What I did not see early on in my ministry is that this is exactly what Jesus was doing with his small group; with his disciples. Jesus was pouring into those 12 disciples in order for them to do the same with other small groups at the opportune time.

This model for equipping the saints and the raising up of good leaders is seen in the apostle Paul's first and second missionary journeys. On his first missionary journey through Asia Minor he shared the gospel, led people to put their faith in Christ and then formed house churches in those communities where the gospel took root. Later, on his second missionary journey when he set out to reach new areas with the gospel he purposefully visited those house churches in Asia Minor in order to further organize them by insuring each house church had a pastor. We are not privy to the particulars of how this was done, but suffice it to say all those small congregations had pastors young in the faith whom Paul had equipped to be able to equip.

It was a memorable day when one of my associates expressed to me their concern that they would have an entire career in vocational ministry and still not have a working definition of what constitutes the making of disciples (Matthew 28:19). I have to admit that his concern suddenly became my concern. So much so I gathered our pastoral staff together for several weekly discussions to try and answer the question of what constitutes the making of a disciple. Each of these meetings lasted a couple of hours as we delved into the Greek language and nuances of the Great Commission. It was after much effort we realized that while we understood the necessity of disciple making we were going to have to learn how it is done by a sheer commitment to seek God's wisdom and direction.

To that point in time (about 13 years into my pastoral ministry) I had only assumed that what we were doing as our tradition with the Sunday school, Sunday morning and evening worship along with Sunday night Discipleship Training as well as Monday night visitation and Wednesday prayer meeting was in fact "making disciples." I do believe that there was some discipleship taking place as a result of these offerings. But the sobering reality was that having all these "opportunities for growth" available was not insuring us that people were actually being equipped and maturing as a result of them. I am assured that a lot of knowledge was gained by our participants but not so confident heart change was taking place.

My associates question launched us on the quest to figure out comprehensively what constitutes the making of a disciple. It has certainly driven us to be much more specific in our aim at "making disciples." We now focus much more on the outcome or evidence of our efforts than to merely be satisfied with making an effort. We are specifically striving to equip the believer on how to live out loud the Christian faith. We have definitely seen believers mature to the point of taking on leadership roles which ultimately contributes to the disciple making ministry of Village Meadows.

Needless to say the question my associate asked those many years ago is still being answered. We are still learning and striving in our efforts at producing growing disciples.

So, what if God raises up exceptional leaders in your church? It will only happen when you establish a disciple making model that actually grows people into maturing believers who actively minister to others.

This is the stuff of fairytales. I mean, who leaves the church money from their inheritance? It is an endless challenge just to get members to give, but an inheritance? Let me say unequivocally that God is the reason and that He uses the foundation of a solid understanding of biblical stewardship as His means through which such a thing could happen.

It is good that there are philanthropists giving from their deep resources to all kinds of organizations and causes. However, when it comes to the most important work in the world, the spreading of the gospel/making disciples, there is the constant strain of needing resources from which to accomplish that. As I have previously noted, Village Meadows has enjoyed some remarkable progress in our efforts to enlarge our campus while reaching more souls for the Kingdom of God. And it is primarily attributed to our emphasis on biblical stewardship.

When a follower of Jesus Christ gets a clear understanding of biblical stewardship they will cherish all the more a church that places a proper emphasis on stewardship. They will support the ministry and be excited as new ministries are proposed and existing ones expanded as a result of increased giving from the members.

I teach what we call the Discovering Village Meadows class which is for those who wish to know more about our church or want to become a member. During that class I teach a short segment on biblical stewardship. As I do I love to call attention to the beautiful campus where we are meeting and highlight the fact that what they see is the result of many members who gave sacrificially through two capital stewardship programs. And that it is sustained by the fact that many of our members understand the biblical mandate to give from what God has blessed them. While I will mention the Scripture on tithing I will add that the sentiment from the New Testament is that the tithe is the starting place from which God would have us steward our resources. It is during this class that I also comment that we are where we are because of church family members giving and not some sugar daddy. I then pause and say that that is about to change with regards to our next building project.

I then proceed to tell them about a man who joined our church some years prior. His name was Bob Stokes. Bob was an unassuming fellow. A retired airline pilot. Dressed in dated clothes that were nice, lived in a decent, but not extravagant home in our city. He did drive a relatively new car. All in all Bob appeared to be comfortable financially but for all one knew he was doing so on a fair pension from the airline along with Social Security. Bob was an avid student of Scripture and consequently understood the demands of being a good steward.

In time Bob would serve on our Stewardship Committee and eventually became a deacon. It was after his death that we discovered how Bob considered his becoming a deacon at Village Meadows the highest honor of his life.

Bob was one of the bravest men I have ever known. Not because he had been a U.S. Marine pilot in the 1950's or had flown commercial airliners his entire career (he loved to say he had a career in the aluminum tubing business) but because of how he faced death. Bob had been a runner. Often you could see him running all over town in his rather bright running shorts. Eventually, though, Bob's age would catch up with him and he would have to stop running. We are talking early eighties by this time. But it was with the onset of lung cancer that Bob would say to me, "I am not going to fight this. I have got more wrong with me than is right and besides, I know where I am going." And so Bob did not fight his cancer and within a little over four months Bob was gone. It would be the day after his passing that something profound about Bob would become evident. He was a multimillionaire.

Bob had prearranged with one of our other deacons to become the executor of his estate (he had been single for 20 years) and instructed him not to open a certain letter until after he had died. It was an incredible moment when Bob's executor called me and told me I needed to come to his house and read the letter Bob had left. In that letter he talked about how his few heirs were going to get a stipend. Enough for his son to buy a house and his two grandkids to pay off college loans. But that he was not going to entrust them with his estate because they refused to follow his counsel on what the Bible teaches on stewardship. Following that he instructed us to pay off the balance of our current debt at the church. And then he wrote, "I think there will be enough remaining to build the new sanctuary."

Our master plan had called for the eventual building of a sanctuary. We had built the first phase for small groups; built a multipurpose building as funds were raised and then the office and utility buildings from proceeds of the sale of the original campus. That left the new sanctuary as the final phase of our master plan but I felt we needed to grow larger before I wanted us to tackle another capital campaign. A new sanctuary was going to be costly.

Bob had been a wise investor. He had been led by the Lord to diversify his investments and to let those investments accrue while only taking funds out to give to those he was led to help out. Much of this came to light in the sharing time at his funeral. Bob left the church the exact amount the IRS will allow to be given a not-for-profit before inheritance tax kicks in—$5.3 million. We paid off our debt of a little less than $500K and set about organizing to build that new sanctuary.

Just so you will know, Bob is not the first member to leave the church some inheritance money. Bob's mom actually left us $100K when she died some years prior. Additionally, in the early '90s the raising of funds to build the new sanctuary at the old campus was stimulated by the leaving of a dear member's inheritance of nearly $250K.

If there is a watchword to all this it would be to think in terms of biblical stewardship and what you can do with your inheritance and the furtherance of the gospel as the end fast approaches.

So, what if a member leaves an inheritance with instructions? First be thankful that God has entrusted your church with the honor of stewarding His resources. Second, take very seriously the fact that the one who left the inheritance thought well enough of the mission of your church to trust you to do God's will with it.

By the way, as of the writing of this it has been six years since we received Bob's inheritance and we are just now seeing the construction of the new sanctuary. That is because God had a lesson we needed to learn first. Read on.

Previously I shared with you the remarkable story of being left with over five million dollars with specific instructions as what to do with it. I did not mention it then, but those instructions saved us a whole lot of grief. Not having to talk about what to do with it kept us from having a multitude of opinions and likely arguments as how to spend it. Nevertheless, we were not saved from other issues arising from this blessing.

I am not going to go into detail here but wanted to at least share with you how having so much money to build a wonderful facility did not exclude God from having a valuable lesson for us in mind. A lesson that would be necessary before He would let us have that new building. The lesson was on the value of people. Namely our immediate neighbors. That regardless their lifestyle, philosophy, or absence of a personal relationship with Jesus Christ, they still matter to God. And that the witness of the church to them matters irrespective of what we see as our rights.

This story begins with a seemingly miraculous opportunity to purchase five acres due west of our campus. It became available just after our architect recommended we purchase it with the intent of putting in another exit which would allow church traffic to move more conveniently off campus. Some years prior we had investigated the possibility of purchasing that land and was met with a rather succinct "absolutely not!" from the owner. It was vacant land with the exception of a work shop the owner had built on site many years prior. The miracle is in the fact that now, some 17 years later, the owner approached us and we purchased it. You can appreciate how we easily concluded it was a God thing. And indeed it was, but interestingly for reasons unforeseen.

As we implemented certain actions to prepare the plot for the new sanctuary we also made some preparations by clearing a portion of that five acres to accommodate the new entrance/exit. It was then that things got real interesting. Knowing that hindsight is 20/20 we should have been in contact with our neighbors regarding these expansion plans. Assuming our existence on this site for the previous ten years would have been enough, our neighbors took exception to this new intrusion into their serenity. These neighbors all live on five acre lots with most of the custom homes being there for many years. While the traffic generated by our new entrance/exit was only going to impact five of those neighbors they were profoundly upset. Since the road upon which they lived was a dead end road there was obviously little traffic and they were not excited about that changing.

I do not slight our neighbors for being upset. Unfortunately two of them confronted two of our members who were doing the clearing. This escalated into a heated argument which became regrettable. I and another pastor went to them and attempted to reason and reconcile with some relative success. However, the devil had already made the most of it.

When one of the neighbors was complaining about the encounter with another neighbor it became the talk of the hood ultimately catching the attention of a young man who was renting a bedroom in a house just to the north of us. His name is Michael and he is about as good an example of a far left liberal as you can find. Michael took it upon himself to get his landlord all riled up over our mistreatment of the neighbors which led to a nasty letter from her. Michael also wrote to me and it was a letter that is hard to describe.

I decided it would be best if I sought out Michael and have a face to face with him. When he was not home I was able to call the number on his letter and made arrangements for him to come to my office and a few days later we met. I was able to share the gospel with him and he acknowledged that he was familiar with it because of an aunt who was Pentecostal. He was not interested in becoming a believer but appeared to be less skeptical. I thought we parted on good terms. Silly me.

Michael set about sending me numerous documents on environmental issues and accusing me of being in it for the money and private jets. O.K. you get the idea. He and a friend thought it important to place door hangers on the area homes just prior to Easter that accused us of being bad for the neighborhood. This actually backfired as we began then to garner sympathy from some neighbors. Even so, Michael continued his campaign by sending disparaging letters to our state convention office and the civil engineering firm working for us. At one point Michael assumed my identity and got me signed up with several solar panel companies. It was disconcerting getting all those sales calls during VBS. This was more than just irritating, it was getting bizarre. Not to say his actions were not already bizarre. I sought the counsel of our deacons and law enforcement and it was decided I needed to be on record with the Sherriff's department. Can you imagine my surprise when they informed me they were already familiar with Michael.

All along I was asking the church to pray for Michael's salvation. We, who are saved, understand better than anyone that without Christ's saving grace so go we.

Once the Sherriff's department was involved things quieted down a bit with just a monthly postal diatribe from Michael instead of weekly one. Then it got interesting again as Michael was avidly involved in anti-Trump rallies in our city. He must have felt some momentum from that and put out on Facebook an invitation for any and every one to join him in picketing Village Meadows Baptist Church. Since he was making this publically known we were prepared for it.

When that Sunday arrived we were able to let the congregation know what they may encounter upon leaving the campus. I asked them to be praying for those who would be picketing and to be sure to smile, wave and wish them God's blessing. One of my staff went down there between services taking cold drinks and engaging them in conversation. He was unable to get them to clearly state why they were there. Interesting.

When I was leaving after our second service I pulled over got out and walked over to talk with them, especially Michael. Of importance is that by the time I got there all seven of them (yes, that is all that showed up) were looking down at the ground and sheepishly avoiding a conversation with me. It was the last I heard from Michael.

It is so important that we take to heart the real meaning behind the command of Christ to turn the other cheek. And, when we do not Satan has a hay-day and the church's witness is harmed. Not to mention an incredible amount of time and energy has to be spent on recovering that witness. All of this served as an invaluable lesson as to the value of people to God. Regardless their behavior.

Satan did his best to use some hurt feelings to break us up but to no avail. That is because doing the right thing and putting people first garners the blessing of God.

By the way, we gave the five acres back to the man we purchased it from. Yes, it cost us some money. But people are more important and in the final analysis we did not need that exit/entrance enough to jeopardize our witness to our neighbors. We decided we value people more than convenience. People matter. Just ask Jesus.

So, what if God teaches you what putting people first really means? When He does it is inevitably painful because of how difficult it is to swallow one's pride. Embrace it and be extremely thankful that God see's you worthy of His discipline and the preservation of your witness to your neighbors.

Late in my pastorate at Rincon Baptist Church in Tucson the Lord opened my eyes to the possibility that our relatively small congregation could actually be the tool God would use to plant another church on the East side. At that time in '95-'96 the way our State Convention promoted church planting was to have a congregation simply agree to be the Mother or sponsor church with somewhat minimal financial obligation. Consequently our church agreed to proceed with the prospects of planting a church in our area of Tucson. I petitioned a number of sister churches in the Catalina Association to partner with us financially and two of them did! This enabled us to have the resources to seek out and eventually move a church planter to Tucson. Along with the Arizona Southern Baptist Convention (ASBC) and North American Mission Board (NAMB) as well as the planter's personal financial support the new work was birthed.

Since arriving at Village Meadows we have had a number of opportunities to plant new works in the Cochise Association and beyond. Some of them have succeeded and some of them have not. Certainly we do not venture into such a proposition with failure on our minds, but suffice it to say that if you do not try you have assured failure.

Of importance to note is how the ASBC in partnership with NAMB have developed a much more ardent and detailed process through which church planters are qualified and heightened expectations of the sponsoring churches. This has led to much greater prospects for a successful and lasting launch.

It is important to understand that being the mechanism or Church sponsor through whom God can raise up a new work is not about being prideful or to have bragging rights. It is about fulfilling the Great Commission (Matthew 28:18-20). Equally important is that it keeps your congregation fully aware of the breadth of such a command in that to fulfill it requires us to step well beyond the walls of the church.

Factored into this mentality is the full-on commitment to be mission-minded. If there is one thing I can point to that has led to the growth and relative ministry successes of Village Meadows is our mission mindedness. Going beyond the importance of giving sacrificially to the Cooperative Program and our annual mission offerings is the exertion of time, talent and resources toward mission action. It is without question that people will give toward ministry they can see and touch. Ministry that takes the person out of the pew and places them on site where a need is strategically addressed.

I know that pastors and congregants can be threatened by the prospects of the financial strain that can come by moving the focus of people and resources away from the demanding needs of keeping the doors open. But I am here to declare that to place your focus on souls in need of the Gospel outside of your geographical area is precisely the attitude God will bless and enable you to, in fact, keep your doors open.

If we expect to be good stewards of what God brings into His storehouse in both people and finances we must apply the full truth of Acts 1:8, *"But you will receive power when the Holy Spirit has come on you, and you will be my witnesses in Jerusalem, in all Judea and Samaria, and to the ends of the earth."*

I want to propose to you that regardless the size of your congregation you can be a part of a church plant. If your congregation is small you seek out other small congregations to partner with, it can be done. There are resources you may not be aware of and all you need do is ask. Contact the church planting strategists through your respective convention office and see what doors and resources that may open and be made available to you. Most importantly communicate well and lead your congregation to be on board. It will be through their ownership and commitment that God will bring the fruit of your efforts toward the birthing of a new congregation where needed.

So, what if God directs you to lead your church to birth another church? Call on the church to pray for a healthy baby. You know, ten toes and ten fingers. What I mean by that is do your homework. Seek the counsel of those who have been called by God to help our churches plant churches. Be actively seeking the necessary resources to succeed. And then, prayerfully follow God as He directs you to a church planter; a location; and others to come along side you and your church.

What if...God wants to use your weaknesses and not your strengths?

As with many works on the subject of church growth and health, as well as church leadership, there is often a component on strength assessment. For you personally and the church collectively knowing your strengths can give greater clarity as to what God would have you give your energies.

When you stop and think about it most of us subconsciously consider our strengths or gift-mix when entertaining the tackling of a project or pursuing a specific ministry. This is not only normal, it is also a wise consideration. But not all of life can be approached this way and in particular the area of obeying God's clear leading when that leading is in opposition to our personal abilities.

There are dozens of examples throughout the Scriptures that tell of those who believed and obeyed when everything within them said run the other way. Of course there are some among those stories who ran first but then repented and obeyed.

I believe you would agree that the norm is to believe that God leads us to pursue the kinds of ministries that are complemented by our gifts or strengths. And that in God's economy there are others whom God will empower and equip to do the things with which you are uncomfortable. While this is normative there are times when God says "go" and you think He's mistaken. That He cannot possibly be telling you to do this or that for the simple fact you do not have the right skill or experiences to qualify.

The story I am about to share with you that demonstrates what I am talking about is not one that involved me directly. This story involves me as a mere observer; an observer of my wife Nancy. The story began just after the worst shooting at a place of worship in American history. It was November 5, 2017, when a lone assassin walked into a small Baptist church in Southerland Springs, Texas, and shot all 46 in attendance leaving 26 fatally wounded. It was in watching the horrific news of that event on television that we learned the pastor and his wife were both out of town on that Sunday, but their 14 year old daughter was present and was one of those who died. Upon hearing that Nancy turned to me and said she felt like God was telling her to go and minister to the pastor's wife of that little country church.

Two things immediately popped into my sometimes overly analytical mind and I said that first of all she would not be able to get within a hundred yards of that pastor's wife. This was easy to conclude when looking at the TV screen and seeing hundreds of people gathered around that pastor and his wife with many of them being either law enforcement, social services or government officials. But even if Nancy could get close enough to her it would likely not be substantive. This had become an international travesty.

The second thing that was on my mind was how Nancy was physically limited due to a medical condition that had rendered her with far less stamina than most of us enjoy. Nancy heeded my logic but God was not letting it go. The following Sunday she asked her small group to pray for her as she explained the strong impression God had put on her heart. The answer to those prayers came quickly as God gave her a letter to write.

Nancy did not have the church's address so she simply addressed it "First Baptist Church, Southerland Springs, Texas 78161, attention Sherri Pomeroy." Sherri was the pastor's wife. Nancy did not really expect a reply since it was anticipated there would be hundreds of thousands of letters from all around the world being sent. Regardless, she was merely doing what she felt God was leading her to do and would craft and send another letter each time God gave her something more to say. On average she would send a letter twice a week and this went on for a little over three months. Then one Friday in late February Nancy felt a letter coming on but I was using the computer, so she decided to look up Sherri on Facebook and messenger her. Much to her surprise Sherri replied saying, "I don't normally accept strangers in this format, but I recognized your name from all the encouraging letters." We later found out that God had directed Sherri to Nancy's letters among the well over a million that had come in. As God was working on this end He was assuredly working on that end.

Let me state the obvious here. When God is clearly leading you to do something, even if it does not make a lot of sense, just understand that He is also working in the lives of those to whom He is directing you.

Nancy continued her letter writing and an occasional encouraging word through private messenger on Facebook. Sherri would often reply to those. Nancy was content that she was doing what God wanted her to do at this point in time. That made sense because by the first of March her level of pain increased causing us to seek a solution from doctors in Tucson but to no avail. After several disappointing conclusions that there was nothing that could be done for Nancy except increased medication, God spoke again. This time it was in late June during the music portion of our Sunday morning service that God said to Nancy, "I told you to go." For the curious we do listen for God to speak to us through His Word and other godly believers. But, we do not typically listen for an inaudible voice from which to get our cues.

When I got home that day Nancy told me of the arresting nature of what God clearly said to her during worship. Regardless the fact that her health was even worse than when God first said "go" I knew it had to be from Him. We both understood that if God is calling He will enable.

As this played out it became obvious that God was going to supply the wherewithal for Nancy to make the trip to Texas and actually spend some time with Sherri at Southerland Springs. It was a life-changing experience for Nancy to make that trip and simply magnified how you do not have to be in perfect health to answer God's call to "go." And neither do you have to possess the skill one would think you would need to befriend someone who has experience the kind of grief that comes from such a tragedy.

When Nancy returned from her trip to Southerland Springs she was overwhelmed how the survivors of that massacre were not angry with God. Rather, they were rejoicing as to where their loved ones now were. In fact, they were busily leading many to faith in Christ. The pastor has led them to commit to and practice Romans 12:21, *"Do not be conquered by evil, but conquer evil with good."* The church has more than tripled in size and what Satan had in mind to destroy a church body only strengthened their resolve to share the good news of Jesus Christ.

Upon hearing about all that God was doing in that church and their determination to bring Him glory I knew we needed to share Nancy's experience with the Village Meadows family. That opportunity to share her story of "When God says go" came two weeks after the first anniversary of the shooting at Southerland Springs and was a true blessing to the congregation. Incredibly, and much to our delight, was how a very special person was in attendance—Sherri Pomeroy. To hear Nancy's testimony go to VillageMeadows.Church, click on the tab "watch" and then on "Sermon Archive," scrolling down to "When God says go").

When God says "go" He may very well be intending to use your weaknesses and not your strengths. And, to take a lesson from the apostle Paul, it may very well be your weaknesses that are the only means with which you can experience God's strength (see 1st Corinthians 12:10).

Nancy went home to be with Jesus on December 6, 2020. She suffered over 19 years from chronic pain. She would often asked why the Lord was allowing her to suffer so. Even still she clung to her Savior and continued to have a ministry of encouragement to dozens whom the Lord led to her. In John 9 Jesus is asked by his disciples who's sin was responsible for the blind man's condition. His response was to say the man's blindness was not from sin but in order for God's works to be displayed in him (v.3). Without question Nancy's condition was for this very purpose. Let what you have just read be a testament to Revelation 14:13 which says, *"Then I heard a voice from heaven saying, 'Write: Blessed are the dead who die in the Lord from now on.' 'Yes,' says the Spirt, 'so they will rest from their labors, since their works follow them.'"*

So, what if God wants to use your weaknesses and not your strengths? Think of possible ways God may be asking you or your congregation to do something that is outside your "comfort zone." Something that you have decided you cannot do because of the lack of resources. Listen, then follow by faith as you sense God's leading.

BIBLICAL RULES OF ORDER
for
VILLAGE MEADOWS BAPTIST CHURCH
Sierra Vista, Arizona

The rules of order for any church body should be solely biblical and founded on the Scriptures. Such as Romans 12:10, *"Show family affection to one another with brotherly love. Outdo one another in showing honor."* Ephesians 4:3, *"diligently keeping the unity of the Spirit with the peace that binds us."* 1st Peter 3:8, *"Now finally, all of you should be like-minded and sympathetic, should love believers, and be compassionate and humble."* And Philippians 2:3-4, *"Do nothing out of rivalry of conceit, but in humility consider others as more important that yourselves. Everyone should look out not only for his own interests, but also for the interests of others."*

This is the character of Christ. There is no arguing in the Trinity. They are not pulling the universe into sectarian camps. We can learn how to walk in these ways. Often it involves dying to self, yielding to Christ, and being patient with one another. Sometimes it means being firm on an absolute unyielding issue, but doing it gently and lovingly. With this biblical model to guide our behavior the over-arching authority to which we submit is captured in Colossians 1:18, *"He is also the head of the body, the church; He is the beginning, the firstborn from the dead, so that He might come to have first place in everything."* Jesus Christ and His teachings serve as our sole model for behavior and decision making.

While the church is bound by the laws of the state to comply with proper accounting methods and if incorporated (which we are) to be organized in such a way as to comply with the state's requirements (the taking of minutes and election of officers), that should be the extent to which the church adheres to man-made rule.

Rather than a humanistic system of decision making involving Robert's Rules of Order and seeking a "majority" vote, the church must desire and follow *Biblical rules of order* as spelled out in God's Word. We must gather in Christ's Name, by His Spirit, treating one another according to the teachings the Scriptures and seeking God's Will in every decision we make. We are brothers and sisters in Christ gathered together in "God's business" to please the Father, being kind and affectionate to one another, giving preference to one another.

When the Holy Spirit has given us oneness, let's guard it in the bond of peace. Let's be careful with one another not to stir up unnecessary strife. Sure the spirit and the flesh war against each other and there will be things within and sometimes among, but let's aim in prayer and faith to be an instrument to avoid it, and not cause it. What a wonderful way to gather, looking for unity and peace. Knowing that God is a Lord of both and He can keep building it.

A majority is not a satisfactory conclusion. We must strive for one-mindedness. "*Live your life in a manner worthy of the gospel of Christ...standing firm in one spirit, <u>with one mind</u>, working side by side for the faith of the gospel.*" (Philippians 1:27) Let's not ask the Lord to get a majority while leaving the minority to feel out of step or worse, failures. Rather, let's ask God to put us all in submission to what He wants to do. And, if we have strong differences it is obviously time for a season of prayer and waiting on the Lord.

Of course there are those exceptions where a member drifts from the Lord and gets into carnality and becomes an obstruction to what God is doing. In those instances God can give wisdom to the body and the naysayer is exposed as one whose negativity is derived from the flesh and not the Spirit.

Should opposition be voiced from more than a mere faction and consequently an agreement cannot be reached by an over-whelming majority, prayer and fasting should be called for until such can be achieved.

1st Peter 5:2 reads, "...*shepherd* [lead] *God's flock among you, not <u>overseeing</u> out of compulsion but freely, according to God's will."* To shepherd means to feed; lead; direct; oversee. The pastor is to care for, lovingly guide and guard the flock entrusted to his care. In an effort to lead the church in a spiritually focused decision making process it is incumbent upon the pastor to lead his flock in humility and as a servant-leader. As such church business meetings should be led by the Pastor. However, under certain circumstances the subject being handled can be perilous for the pastor in that it can appear to be self-serving. Such can be the case with budget adoption meetings or with new staff proposals and it will be wiser for the chair of the appropriate committee or ministry team to lead the discussion and ensuing vote/affirmation.

ACTS 15
A fundamental example of the *Biblical Rules of Order* are the first three "business meetings" recorded in Acts. Acts 1:12-26 shows the process in its infancy where the apostles gather with others (120) to decide on how best to fill the apostolic vacancy left by Judas Iscariot. In *agreement* they select two candidates and then cast lots to decide which one it was to be (do not forget the church is in its infancy).

In Acts 6 the apostles recommended to the whole assembly that they chose seven men of good report to serve the needs of the church. *"It pleased the whole body..."* (v.5)

Then in Acts 15, when Paul and Barnabas propose to the church at Jerusalem the inclusion of Gentiles into the body of faith the steps are clearly laid out. Verses 1-4 are about the proposal. Verse 5 is about some opposition followed with much discussion (vv.6-7a). Verses 7b-12 record how Peter, then Barnabas and Paul speak to the issue. Then in verses 13-21 we see how James, the pastor of the Jerusalem church, speaks to the matter and makes his recommendation. Verse 22 then tells of the unanimity among the church in its decision to invite the Gentile believers into the family of faith.

The heart of the whole process is recorded in verse 28, *"For it was the Holy Spirit is decision—and ours…"* Seeking God's will <u>through the Spirit of Christ</u> should and must be the rules of order by which we carry out the business of His church.

Submitted by Pastor Mark Pitts and approved by the Church Council, June 13, 2010, then adopted by the Church, September 26, 2010.

The "One Another's" of the Church Family

Love one another – John 13:34

Serve one another - Galatians 5:13

Bear one another's burdens - Galatians 6:2

Honor one another - Romans 12:10

Show family affection to one another – Romans 12:10

Submit to one another - Ephesians 5:21

Be at peace with one another – Mark 9:50

Be in agreement with one another – Romans 12:16

Live in harmony with one another – Romans 15:5

Accept one another - Romans 15:7

Instruct one another – Romans 15:14

Greet one another - Romans 16:16

Bear with one another – Ephesians 4:2

Be kind and compassionate to one another –
Ephesians 4:32

Forgive one another - Colossians 3:13

Admonish one another – Colossians 3:16

Encourage one another – 1st Thessalonians 5:11

Appendix III

Having seen the unfortunate fallout that comes from a poor understanding of the deacon's role in Scripture I have often wondered how that is possible. If we are serious about following God's revealed Word in Scripture then the answer may be in forgetting that verses 1-7 and 8-13 In 1st Timothy 3 have to do with a life in *subjection* to the lordship of Jesus Christ. When we do that it is far too easy to interpret them as having something to do with an authoritative role in the church. To do so is to ignore the purpose for that criterion. Reading all of 1st Timothy we can see that Paul's overriding theme is about humble servitude, not about who is in charge.

As was noted earlier, the only significant distinction between the two sets of conditions for pastors and deacons is that the pastor (*poimen*) is to be an able teacher. Other than that, Paul purposefully connects the criteria for pastors to the criteria for deacons with the word "likewise" in v.8. In so doing the apostle infers that the descriptions given for the pastor are in sync with those of the deacon. Again, if there is an eye on who gets to be in charge the interpreter will miss the point for the criteria to be a deacon.

On the matter of leadership the mere distinction between *diakonos* and *poimen* is sufficient. As has been established *diakonos* (deacon) defines one who serves while *poimen* (pastor) literally means one who feeds.

Pastors are to feed the flock and consequently the ones who feed are also the ones who lead.

Does this mean that deacons cannot lead? Not in the least, but that leadership is not in a biblically authoritative vain as is seen in other passages relating to the duties of the pastor. Rather, I see the deacon's leadership taking place through his humble service to the pastor(s). Therefore, when it comes to those who bear the title of "deacon" their role in that particular capacity is to minister to the needs of the pastors of the church.

Concerning the modern day deacon nothing has fundamentally changed from the 1st century—his function is to free up the pastor to be in prayer and sermon/Bible teaching preparation. With respect to the other ordained pastors on staff the same applies. With this in mind it becomes profoundly clear that the deacon's role has as much to do with the equipping ministry of the church as anyone else—freeing the pastoral staff to pray and prepare/equip the church body for ministry.

But the question remains: "How does the deacon 'serve' the pastor?" While Acts 6 pulls our attention toward some physical intervention (feeding the Hellenist widows) I believe the early church understood God's intent for these special servants was far more spiritual. Acts 6 has traditionally been interpreted with a focus on what the deacons did and not why they did it. While it was a service to the Greek widows it was a spiritual act for and to the pastors. This is why I believe the Holy Spirit guided Paul to give us 1st Timothy 3.

This is a major paradigm shift in our understanding of the deacon's role in the church. From this perspective we begin to realize that the deacon's primary focus was directed toward the needs of the pastor(s) which in the particular instance of Acts 6 resulted in a ministry action of service to some in need within the church.

If the deacon's primary function is to protect/provide/assist the pastor then it may be best understood that at a minimum the deacon's role is to serve as a *spiritual shield* to the pastor(s). Instead of the focus being on the needs of people in the church the focus is on the needs of the pastor. Granted, just as in Acts 6, this can result in some practical, hands on intervention to allow the pastor to pursue his calling, but that is only a small part of pastoral care. The larger part is carried out in the trenches of intercessory prayer, peace making, encouraging all to minister to one another, by being a sounding board, and giving counsel or affirmation to the pastor.

Something I have learned is that when you have a staff and some of them are fellow pastors the tendency is to look to them as your sounding board and counselors. Nothing wrong with that but you miss some important insights the deacons can offer you if you fail to act upon their calling to be ready advisors. There is a distinction between the way vocational leaders communicate to you and deacons. Deacons have the perspective of the laity and their input is crucial in the decision making process.

A Final Observation

Regarding deacon's wives the Scripture leaves no confusion that the wives of the deacon are to be *"worthy of respect, not slanderers, self-controlled, faithful in everything"* (1st Timothy 3:11). As I mentioned before when Paul linked the two sets of criteria together with the word "likewise" he was synchronizing the two. In other words what is expected of the deacon's wife should be expected of the pastor's wives.

Given the fact that our wives are expected to come under and satisfy the same scrutiny it is therefore reasonable to view them just as called to this particular work and true help-mates in our respective roles.